D1085782

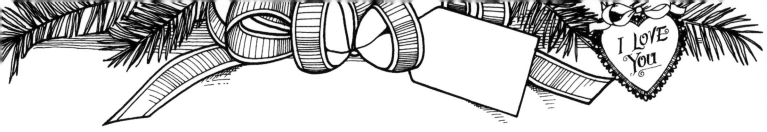

The Anti-Coloring Book® of Celebrations

Susan Striker

Illustrations by Sally Schaedler

An Owl Book

Henry Holt and Company

New York

Thanks to:
Esther Banker, Byram Shubert Library
Nikki and Sue Frano
Mary Meeker, New Lebanon School Media Center
Masako Nakagawa
Carol Terwilliger
Lyles Williams

This book is dedicated to Bob,
who appreciates family holidays and traditions as much as I do.
With thanks for all those mushy cards and lovely gifts
and for always remembering.

Henry Holt and Company, Inc.
Publishers since 1866
115 West 18th Street
New York, New York 10011

Henry Holt® is a registered
trademark of Henry Holt and Company, Inc.

ISBN 0-8050-3414-5

Henry Holt books are available for special
promotions and premiums.
For details contact:
Director, Special Markets.

First Edition—1995

Designed by Paula R. Szafranski

Printed in the United States of America
All first editions are printed on acid-free paper. ∞

1   3   5   7   9   10   8   6   4   2

Introduction

I have always loved holidays! Perhaps it is because I was born on Christmas Eve. My sister's birthday is just four days later, and it seemed only fair to us that schools were always closed that week! I was married on Columbus Day, so my husband and I have a three-day anniversary celebration every year. I lost my mother on Bastille Day, and the fireworks and parades in France each summer seem to me to be in honor of her memory. Holidays help us remember special occasions in our families as well as in history, marking special moments in time. They also give us an opportunity to create new memories, from the beginning of our lives to the end. Holidays offer the chance to enjoy flowers, gifts, balloons, good food, and bear hugs and kisses from loved ones. We step away from the routine of work and school to spend time with family and friends and to reflect on the meaning of the milestone. Holidays provide the basis for the traditions of our families and our culture. They also bring distant family members together.

Unfortunately, too often we present children with holiday art projects that have more to do with stereotypes and patterns than they do with the true meaning of the day. Instead of taking the time to reflect with our children each Thanksgiving on the many things we have to be grateful for, we tell them to trace around their hands, paste down a few feathers and encourage them to see this poor excuse for children's art as a drawing of a turkey. And once presented with the cliché, children often accept it forever, never stopping to realize how little it resembles a real bird or how little that bird has to do with the true meaning of the holiday. Trace a red heart each Valentine's Day instead of really expressing yourself and your love; make some black triangle eyes on a perfectly round orange pumpkin and never stop to think that pumpkins never grow as perfect circles; make a green triangle to represent an evergreen tree each Christmas; and each St. Patrick's Day, be sure to pull out the shamrock pattern. The list goes on and on, and such stereotypes have turned more children away from creative thinking than anything else I know of.

Holidays are exciting. They can be fun to look forward to and interesting to reflect on. In short, they provide all the motivation for a sound and meaningful art experience. Celebrations expose children to new situations, help them establish their place in society, and teach them the importance of tradition. This is the first Anti-Coloring Book® in the series in which I suggest books young people may like to read, as we do in my classroom, to enhance and enrich the art experience. I have also supplied a holiday to enjoy every day, so pick one out from the perpetual calendar and celebrate!*

Happy Holidays!

Susan Striker

*To learn more about some of these special days, look at *Chase's Calendar of Events* (Chicago: Contemporary Books, 1994).

• JANUARY •

1st - New Year's Day
2nd - Kakizome (celebrates traditional brush strokes) in Japan
3rd - Congress Assembles
4th - Louis Braille's Birthday (1809)
5th - Twelfth Night
6th - Carnival Season Begins
7th - Galileo Discovered the Moons of Jupiter (1610)
8th - Women's Day in Greece
9th - National Clean Up Your Desk Day
10th - First Meeting of UN General Assembly
11th - National Thank You Day
12th - Hal 3 Computer (in the movie *2001*) Born
13th - Blame Someone Else Day
14th - End of American Revolutionary War
15th - Martin Luther King's Birthday (1929)
16th - National Nothing Day
17th - Anniversary of Organization of PTA
18th - Pooh Day—A. A. Milne's Birthday (1882)
19th - Edgar Allen Poe's Birthday (1809)
20th - Sun Enters Aquarius
21st - National Hugging Day
22nd - National Popcorn Day
23rd - New Year Celebration in China (date varies)
24th - Gold Discovery in California (1848)
25th - A Room of One's Own Day
26th - Australia Day
27th - Backward Day
28th - National Kazoo Day
29th - National Puzzle Day
30th - Muhammed's Birthday (570)
31st - National Handwriting Day

• FEBRUARY •

1st - National Freedom Day
2nd - Groundhog Day
3rd - Bob Leiner's Birthday
4th - Halfway Point of Winter
5th - Constitution Day in Mexico
6th - Midwinter Celebration
7th - Ballet Introduced to the U.S.
8th - Ha-Ri Ku-Yo (Needle Mass) in Japan
9th - National Kraut and Frank Week Begins
10th - "All the News That's Fit to Print" logo first used by *The New York Times*
11th - Youth Day in Cameroon
12th - World Marriage Day
13th - Grant Wood's Birthday (1892)
14th - Valentine's Day
15th - Harold Arlen's Birthday (1905)
16th - Cultural Diversity Day, Westboro, Mass.
17th - Raphael Peale's Birthday (1774)
18th - Louis Comfort Tiffany's Birthday (1848)
19th - Copernicus's Birthday (1473)
20th - Sun Enters Pisces
21st - Lailat al-Qadr (date varies)
22nd - George Washington's Birthday (1732)
23rd - Charro Days in Brownsville, Tex.
24th - Winslow Homer's Birthday (1836)
25th - Pierre Auguste Renoir's Birthday (1841)
26th - Honoré Daumier's Birthday (1808)
27th - Henry Wadsworth Longfellow's Birthday (1882)
28th - Mardi Gras (date varies)

• MARCH •

1st - Youth Art Month Begins
2nd - Dr. Seuss's Birthday (1904)
3rd - I Want You to Be Happy Day
4th - Constitution Day
5th - International Day of the Seal
6th - Michelangelo Buonarroti's Birthday (1475)
7th - Salvador Dali Museum Opened, St. Petersburg, Fla.
8th - UN International Women's Day
9th - Panic Day
10th - Telephone Was Invented
11th - Johnny Appleseed Day
12th - Girl Scouts of America Founded
13th - Most Boring Film Award Given
14th - Albert Einstein's Birthday (1879)
15th - Ides of March
16th - Freedom of Information Day
17th - St. Patrick's Day
18th - Camp Fire Boys and Girls Founded
19th - Swallows Return to Capistrano
20th - Benito Juarez's Birthday (1806)
21st - First Day of Spring
22nd - Rosa Bonheur's Birthday (1822)
23rd - Liberty Day (Anniversary of Patrick Henry's Speech, 1775)
24th - Epstein Young Artists Program Anniversary
25th - Pecan Day
26th - Robert Frost's Birthday (1874)
27th - Edward Steichen's Birthday (1879)
28th - National Organize Your Home Office Day
29th - Vietnam Veterans' Day
30th - Francisco de Goya's Birthday (1746)
31st - Eiffel Tower Anniversary

• APRIL •

1st - April Fool's Day
2nd - International Children's Book Day
3rd - Chicken Little Awards Given
4th - Maya Angelou's Birthday (1928)
5th - Tomb Sweeping Day in Taiwan
6th - Raphael's Birthday (1483)
7th - No Housework Day
8th - Hana Matsuri (Flower Festival) in Japan
9th - Martyrs' Day
10th - Humane Day
11th - Barbershop Quartet Day
12th - Thank You School Library Day
13th - Songkran Day in Thailand
14th - Pan American Day
15th - Thomas Hart Benton's Birthday (1889)
16th - Wilbur Wright's Birthday (1867)
17th - Leonardo da Vinci's Birthday (1452)
18th - National Youth Service Day
19th - Day of the Indian in Venezuela
20th - Sun Enters Taurus
21st - Earth Day
22nd - First Arbor Day, Nebraska 1872
23rd - William Shakespeare's Birth and Death Anniversary (1564–1616)
24th - Edmund Cartwright's Birthday (1743)
25th - Portugal Day
26th - John James Audubon's Birthday (1785)
27th - Take Your Daughter to Work Day
28th - National Arbor Day
29th - Louisiana First Bloom Festival
30th - May Day Eve

• MAY •

1st - Hawaii Lei Day
2nd - Leonardo da Vinci Died (1519)
3rd - Tin Hau Festival in Hong Kong
4th - Relationship Renewal Day
5th - Cinco de Mayo in Mexico
6th - Astronomy Day
7th - Paste-up Day
8th - No Socks Day
9th - National Bike to Work Day
10th - National Tourist Appreciation Day
11th - Salvador Dali's Birthday (1904)
12th - Limerick Day
13th - Jamestown Day USA
14th - Underground America Day
15th - Jasper Johns's Birthday (1930)
16th - Wear Purple for Peace Day
17th - Segregation in U.S. Public Schools Ends (1954)
18th - International Museum Day
19th - Youth Day in Turkey
20th - Frank Lloyd Wright Celebration, Oak Park, Ill.
21st - Albrecht Dürer's Birthday (1471)
22nd - Mary Cassatt's Birthday (1845)
23rd - Labour Day in Jamaica
24th - Portrait Painter James Peale Died
25th - National Missing Children's Day
26th - Sylvia Glaser's Birthday
27th - Children's Day in Nigeria
28th - Memorial Day in Puerto Rico
29th - John F. Kennedy's Birthday (1917)
30th - Memorial Day
31st - Walt Whitman's Birthday (1819)

• JUNE •

1st - Children's Festival Day in China
2nd - Youth Day in Tunisia
3rd - Memorial to Broken Dolls Day in Japan
4th - Day of the Rice God in Japan
5th - UN World Environment Day
6th - Flag Day in Sweden
7th - Paul Gauguin's Birthday (1848)
8th - Frank Lloyd Wright's Birthday (1867)
9th - Donald Duck's Birthday
10th - Maurice Sendak's Birthday (1928)
11th - Jeannette Rankin (First U.S. Congresswoman) Born
12th - Helsinki Day in Finland
13th - National Clay Week Begins
14th - Flag Day
15th - Artist and Cartoonist Saul Steinberg's Birthday
16th - 1st Baseball Ladies Day
17th - Hog Day
18th - Father's Day (date varies)
19th - World Sauntering Day
20th - Flag Day in Argentina
21st - First Day of Summer
22nd - Schoolteachers' Day in El Salvador
23rd - Midsummer's Day
24th - Celebration of the Senses
25th - Log Cabin Day in Michigan
26th - UN International Day Against Drug Abuse
27th - Helen Keller's Birthday (1880)
28th - Peter Paul Rubens's Birthday (1577)
29th - Tatanka Festival Honoring Buffalo in North Dakota
30th - Leap Second Adjustment Time

• JULY •

1st - Anti-Boredom Month Begins
2nd - Midpoint of Year at Noon
3rd - First day of "Dog Days," the 40 Hottest Days in Northern Hemisphere
4th - Independence Day in the U.S.
5th - P. T. Barnum's Birthday (1810)

6th - First All-Star Major League Baseball Game (1933)
7th - Tanahata (Star Festival) in Japan
8th - Anniversary of First Passport Issued
9th - Independence Day in Argentina
10th - Independence Day in the Bahamas
11th - UN World Population Day
12th - Video Games Day
13th - Night Watch in France
14th - Bastille Day in France
15th - St. Swithin's Day in the United Kingdom
16th - National Ice Cream Day
17th - "Wrong Way" Crossing Day
18th - Day of National Mourning
19th - Edgar Degas's Birthday (1834)
20th - First Man Landed on Moon
21st - Independence Day in Belgium
22nd - "Pied Piper of Hamelin" Anniversary
23rd - Soma No Umaoi (Wild Horse Chasing Festival) in Japan
24th - Valencia Fair in Spain
25th - Independence Day in The Netherlands
26th - Revolution Day in Cuba
27th - Walk Your Houseplants Day
28th - Independence Day in Peru
29th - Feast of St. Olaf
30th - Marseillaise Day in France
31st - Take Your Pet to School Day

• AUGUST •

1st - Fiesta Day in Nicaragua
2nd - Kids' Day in Baltimore
3rd - The First Week in August Is National Smile Week
4th - Peer Gynt Festival in Norway
5th - Teddy Bear Rally, Amherst, Mass.
6th - Friendship Day
7th - Halfway Point of Summer
8th - Andy Warhol's Birthday (1927)
9th - Independence Day in Singapore
10th - Independence Day in Ecuador
11th - Independence Day in Chad
12th - Youth Day in Zambia
13th - International Left-handers Day
14th - Liberty Tree Day in Massachusetts
15th - Independence Day in India
16th - Artists in the Park Day in Wolfeboro, N.H.
17th - Larry Rivers's Birthday (1923)
18th - Bad Poetry Day
19th - Candlelight Vigil for Homeless Animals
20th - Eero Saarinen's Birthday (1910)
21st - Hawaii Statehood Anniversary (1959)
22nd - Be an Angel Day
23rd - Sun Enters Virgo
24th - Vesuvius Day in Italy
25th - Kiss and Make Up Day
26th - Women's Equality Day
27th - Wedding of the Giants Day in Belgium
28th - Dream Day
29th - "Playing by the Rules" Day
30th - Feast Day of St. Rose in Peru
31st - Independence Day in Trinidad and Tobago

• SEPTEMBER •

1st - Bumbershoot Art Festival Begins, Seattle
2nd - Artquake Festival Begins in Portland, Ore.
3rd - Gondola Regatta Festival in Venice

4th - Huckleberry Finn Raft Race
5th - Be Late for Something Day
6th - National Do It! Day
7th - Grandma Moses's Birthday (1860)
8th - UN International Literacy Day
9th - Federal Lands Cleanup Day
10th - Swap Ideas Day
11th - No News Is Good News Day
12th - Respect for the Aged Day in Japan
13th - The Star-Spangled Banner Written
14th - International Cross-Culture Day
15th - National Hispanic Heritage Month
16th - Sand Sculpture Contest, Biloxi, Miss.
17th - Citizenship Day
18th - National Youth of the Year Day
19th - U.S. International Day of Peace
20th - "Jelly Roll" Morton's Birthday (1885)
21st - Confucius's Birthday (551 B.C.)
22nd - Ice Cream Cone Invented by Italo Marchiony (1903)
23rd - First Day of Autumn
24th - National Good Neighbor Day
25th - First American Newspaper Published (1690)
26th - T. S. Eliot's Birthday (1888)
27th - Ancestor Appreciation Day
28th - Cartoonist Al Capp's Birthday (1909)
29th - Sundown Dance, Taos, N. Mex.
30th - Babe Ruth Hits 60th Home Run, 1927 Season

• OCTOBER •

1st - Adopt a Dog at a Local Shelter Month
2nd - Mohandas Gandhi's Birthday (1869)
3rd - Norway Pageantry in Oslo
4th - Ten-Four Day Honoring Radio Operators
5th - Republic Day in Portugal
6th - American Library Association Founded (1876)
7th - Fire Prevention Week (date varies)
8th - Sukkot Begins (date varies)
9th - Discoverers' Day in Hawaii
10th - Double Tenth Day
11th - Susan Striker's Wedding Anniversary (1992)
12th - Columbus Day
13th - National School Celebration
14th - Be Bald and Be Free Day
15th - National Grouch Day
16th - Dictionary Day in Honor of Noah Webster
17th - Black Poetry Day
18th - Alaska Day Festival
19th - Evaluate Your Life Day
20th - Kenyatta Day in Kenya
21st - Make a Difference Day
22nd - Robert Rauschenberg's Birthday (1925)
23rd - Inventor Nicolas Appert's Birthday (c. 1750)
24th - United Nations Day
25th - Pablo Picasso's Birthday (1881)
26th - Horseless Carriage Day
27th - Roy Lichtenstein's Birthday (1923)
28th - Jonas Salk's Birthday (1914)
29th - U.S. Stock Market Crash (1929)
30th - Alfred Sisley's Birthday (1899)
31st - Halloween

• NOVEMBER •

1st - National Authors Day
2nd - Day of the Dead in Mexico
3rd - Jason Striker's Birthday (1979)
4th - Sadie Hawkins Day

5th - Hug a Bear Day (date varies)
6th - Saxophone Day
7th - Halfway Point of Autumn
8th - X Ray Discovery Day
9th - Stanford White's Birthday (1853)
10th - William Hogarth's Birthday (1764)
11th - Veterans' Day
12th - Auguste Rodin's Birthday (1840)
13th - Robert Louis Stevenson's Birthday (1850)
14th - Claude Monet's Birthday (1840)
15th - National Young Readers' Day
16th - Great American Smokeout
17th - Homemade Bread Day
18th - Mickey Mouse's Birthday (1928)
19th - Have a Bad Day Day
20th - Astronomer Edwin Hubble's Birthday (1889)
21st - World Hello Day
22nd - National Stop the Violence Day
23rd - Sun Enters Sagittarius
24th - Benedict de Spinoza's Birthday (1632)
25th - Shopping Reminder Day (only 1 month until Christmas)
26th - Presidential Proclamation of First Thanksgiving
27th - Chiam Weizmann's Birthday (1874)
28th - William Blake's Birthday (1827)
29th - Louisa May Alcott's Birthday (1832)
30th - Statue of Ramses II Unearthed (1991)

• DECEMBER •

1st - World AIDS Day
2nd - Georges Pierre Seurat's Birthday (1859)
3rd - Gilbert Stuart's Birthday (1755)
4th - Day of the Artisans
5th - National Day in Thailand
6th - Alfred Eisenstaedt's Birthday (1898)
7th - Pearl Harbor Day
8th - Diego Rivera's Birthday (1886)
9th - Independence Day in Tanzania
10th - Human Rights Day
11th - UNICEF Anniversary
12th - 12th Day of the 12th Month
13th - St. Lucia Day in Sweden
14th - Nostradamus's Birthday (1503)
15th - Halcyon Days Begin
16th - Ludwig von Beethoven's Birthday (1770)
17th - Anniversary of First Wright Brothers' Flight
18th - Feast of Our Lady of Solitude in Mexico
19th - Lailat al-Miraj
20th - Sacagawea's Death Anniversary
21st - Winter Solstice
22nd - Sun Enters Capricorn
23rd - Feast of Radishes in Mexico
24th - Christmas Eve
25th - Christmas
26th - Boxing Day in Canada
27th - Radio City Music Hall Opened (1932)
28th - Helen Frankenthaler's Birthday
29th - Most Dubious News Stories of the Year Day
30th - Rizal Day
31st - Check Smoke Alarms Day

Martin Luther King, Jr., had a dream for the future. What is your dream for the future?

I have a dream that my four children will one day live in a nation where they will not be judged by the color of their skin but by the content of their character.

—Dr. Martin Luther King, Jr.

Martin Luther King
Words by Rosemary L. Bray
Paintings by Malchah Zehdis
(New York: Greenwillow Books, 1995)

I have a dream that:_____

_____

_____

_____

Make a secret
the candles on

wish as you blow out
your birthday cake.

The Wish

Each birthday wish
I've ever made
Really does come true.
Each year I wish
I'll grow some more
And every year
I do!
—Ann Friday

From *Birthdays Rhymes, Special Times*
Selected by Bobbye S. Goldstein
(New York: Doubleday Books for
Young Readers, 1993)

Make a Wish, Molly
Barbara Cohen
Illustrated by Jan Naimo Jones
(New York: Doubleday Books for
Young Readers, 1994)

©Susan Striker

Valentine's Day Grump
Rose Greydanus
Illustrated by Don Page
(New York: Troll Associates,
1981)

Cranberry Valentine
Wende and Harry Devlin
(New York: Four Winds Press, 1986)

The Best Valentine in the World
Marjorie Weinman Sharmat
Illustrated by Lilian Obligado
(New York: Holiday House,
1982)

©Susan Striker

Make a valentine

for someone who really needs one.

Celebrate! March Is Youth Art Month

Hattie and the Wild Waves
Story and pictures by
Barbara Cooney
(New York: Viking, 1990)

The Art Lesson
Tomie de Paola
(New York: G. P.
Putnam's Sons, 1989)

Francie's Paper Puppy
Achim Broger
Illustrated by Michele Sambin
(New York: Alphabet Press, 1984)

Pearl Paints
Abigail Thomas
Illustrated by
Margaret Hewitt
(New York: Henry Holt,
1994)

©Susan Striker

T'Bu'Shvat and Arbor Day are both celebrated by planting trees. Join the celebrations and plant a tree in your community to commemorate these holidays.

The Ghost-Eye Tree
Bill Martin, Jr.
Illustrated by Ted Rand
(New York: Henry Holt, 1985)

The Willow Maiden
Meghan Collins
and Laszlo Gal
(New York: Dial Books for Young Readers, 1985)

Birches
Robert Frost
Illustrated by Ed Young
(New York: Henry Holt, 1988)

The Giving Tree
Shel Silverstein
(New York: HarperCollins, 1964)

Create your own kite for Takoage Taikai, the Japanese kite festival.

Kite Flier/Dennis Hascly
Illustrated by David Wiesner
(New York: Macmillan, 1986)

Japanese Boys' Festival/Janet Riehecky
(Chicago: Children's Press, 1994)

Sofie's Role/Amy Heath and Sheila Hamanaka
(New York: Four Winds Press, 1992)

The Easter Egg Farm
Written and illustrated by
Mary Jane Auch
(New York: Holiday
House, 1992)

✳

Rechenka's Eggs
Patricia Polacco
(New York:
Philomel Books, 1988)

The Easter bunny hid the eggs you decorated for the egg hunt.

The Olympics
Peter Tatlow
(New York:
Bookwright Press, 1988)

The first modern Olympics Games were held on April 6, 1896. Picture yourself participating in your favorite sport.

©Susan Striker

My Mother Is the
Most Beautiful Woman in the World
Becky Reyher/Illustrated by Ruth Gannett
(New York: Lothrop, Lee &
Shepard Books, 1945)

Jafta's Mother
Hugh Lewin
Illustrated by
Lisa Kopper
(Minneapolis:
Carolrhoda
Books, 1988)

I Love My Mommy Because . . .
Laurel Porter-Gaylord
(New York: Dutton, 1991)

What is your favorite thing about Mom?
. . . and your least favorite?

Weird Parents
Audrey Wood
(New York: Dial Books for
Young Readers, 1990)

My Wicked Stepmother
Norman Leach
Illustrated by Jane Browne
(New York: Macmillan, 1993)

The Trouble with Mom
Babette Cole
(New York: Putnam's, 1986)

My Dad the Magnificent
Kristy Parker
Illustrated by Lillian Hoban
(New York: E. P. Dutton, 1987)

I Love My Daddy Because . . .
Laurel Porter-Gaylord/Ashley Wolff
(New York: Dutton Children's Books, 1991)

On Father's Day, think about what you love best about an important man in your life . . .

What Mary Jo Shared
Janice May Udry
Illustrated by Eleanor Mill
(Chicago: Scott, Foresman, 1966)

Jafta's Father
Hugh Lewin
Illustrated by Lisa Kopper
(Minneapolis: Carolrhoda Books, 1983)

. . . and what makes you angriest.

Goals

As you graduate, look forward to your future.

I Want to Be
Thylias Moss and
Jerry Pinkney
(New York: Dial Books for
Young Readers, 1993)

*Zora Hurston and the
Chinaberry Tree*
William Miller/Illustrated
by Cornelius Van Wright
and Ying-Hwa Hu
(New York:
Lee and Low
Books, 1994)

What do you like best about the very first day at the beach each summer?

Morning Beach
Leslie Baker
(Boston: Little, Brown, 1990)

My Island Grandma
Kathryn Lasky and Amy Schwartz
(New York: Morrow Junior Books, 1993)

Until I Saw the Sea
Collected and illustrated by
Alison Shaw
(New York: Henry Holt,
1995)

For National Library Week, list a few of your favorite books and draw an illustration about the very best.

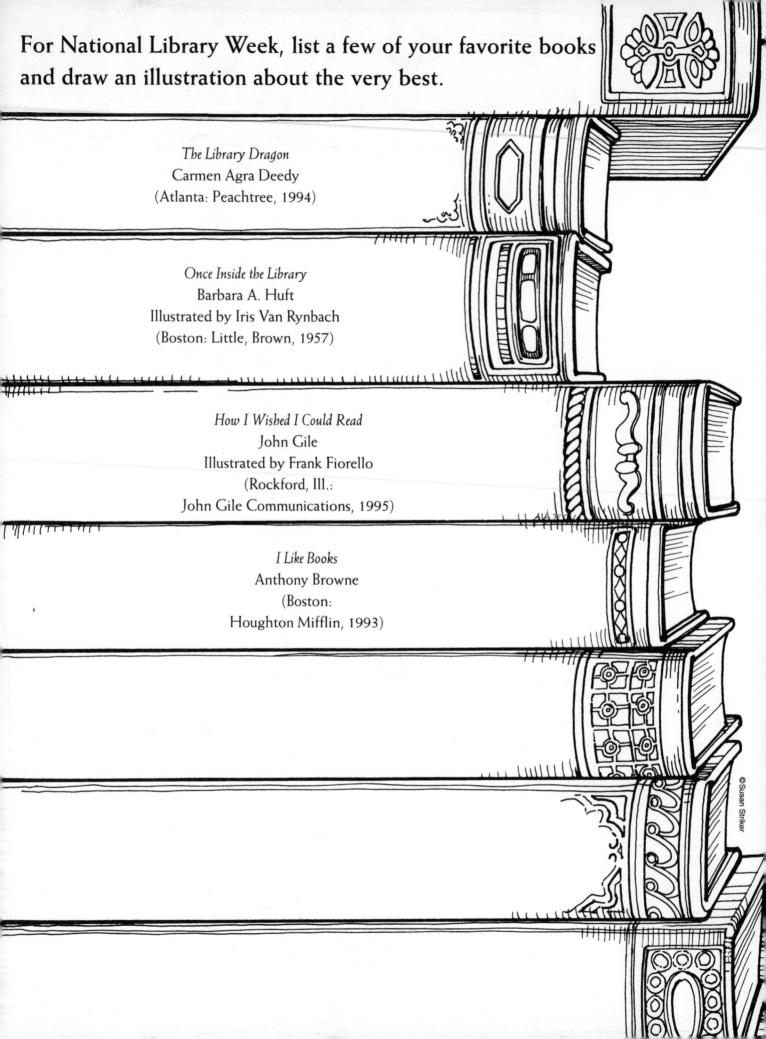

The Library Dragon
Carmen Agra Deedy
(Atlanta: Peachtree, 1994)

Once Inside the Library
Barbara A. Huft
Illustrated by Iris Van Rynbach
(Boston: Little, Brown, 1957)

How I Wished I Could Read
John Gile
Illustrated by Frank Fiorello
(Rockford, Ill.:
John Gile Communications, 1995)

I Like Books
Anthony Browne
(Boston:
Houghton Mifflin, 1993)

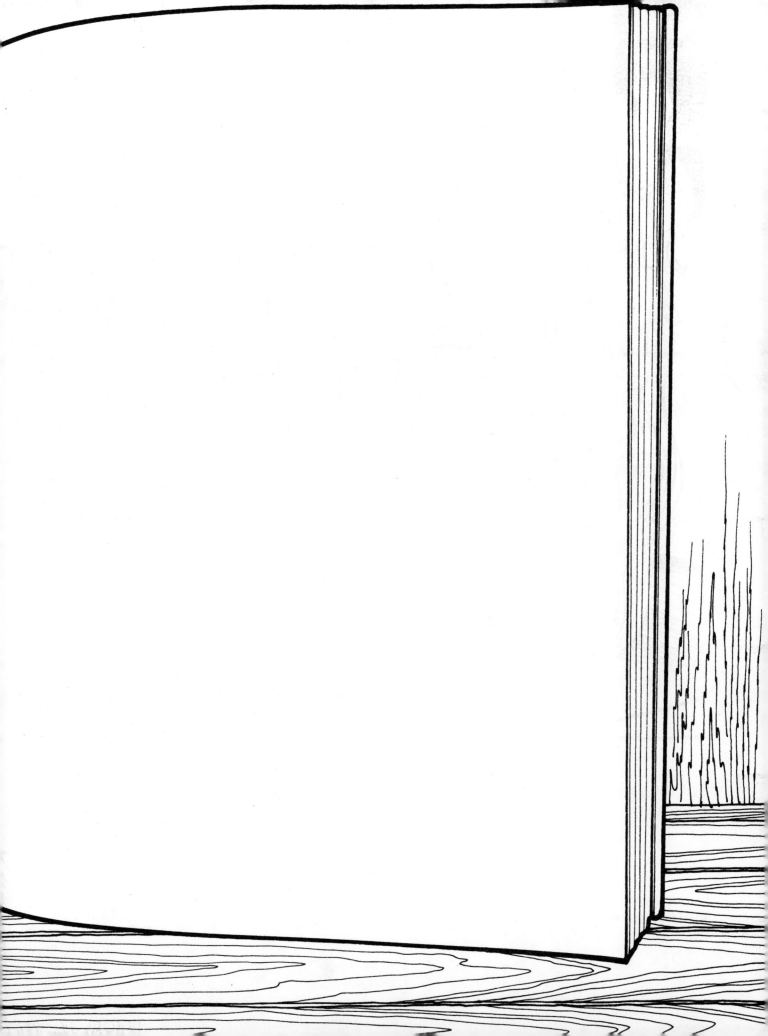

Fourth of July Bear
Kathryn Lasky and Helen
Cogancherry
(New York:
Morrow Junior Books,
1991)

Thump, Thump, Rat-a-Tat-Tat
Gene Baer/Illustrated by
Lois Ehlert
(New York: HarperCollins,
1989)

Parade
Tom Shachtman
Photographs by Chuck Saaf
(New York: Macmillan,
1985)

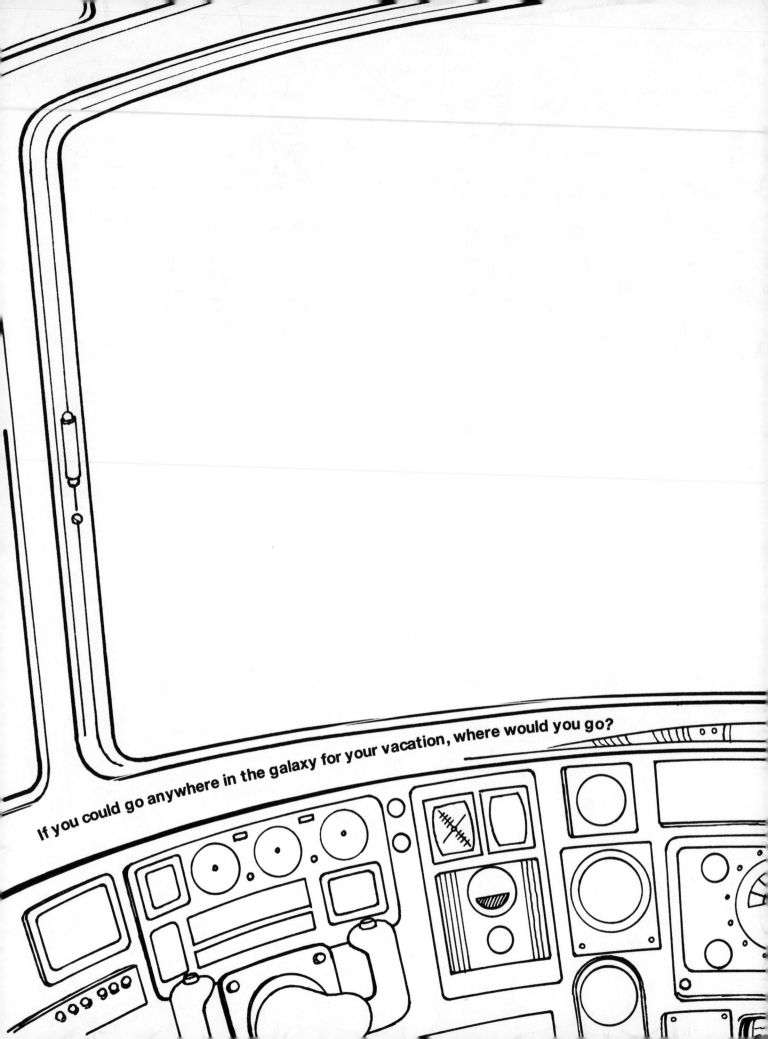

If you could go anywhere in the galaxy for your vacation, where would you go?

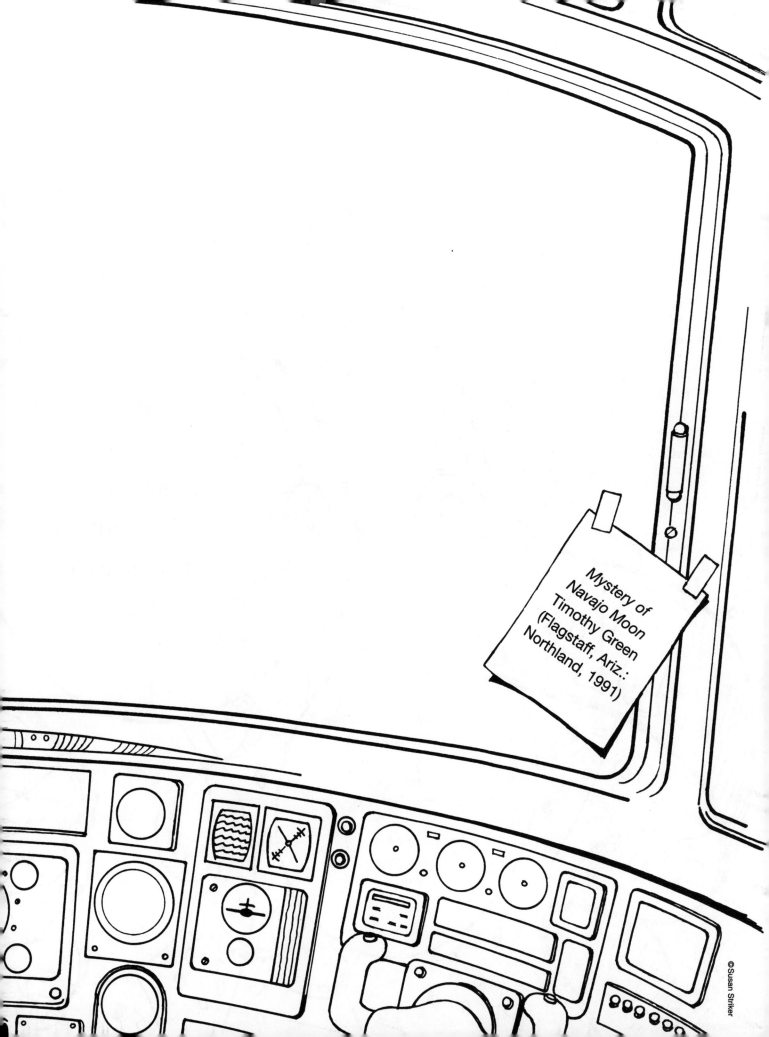

Mystery of
Navajo Moon
Timothy Green
(Flagstaff, Ariz.:
Northland, 1991)

©Susan Striker

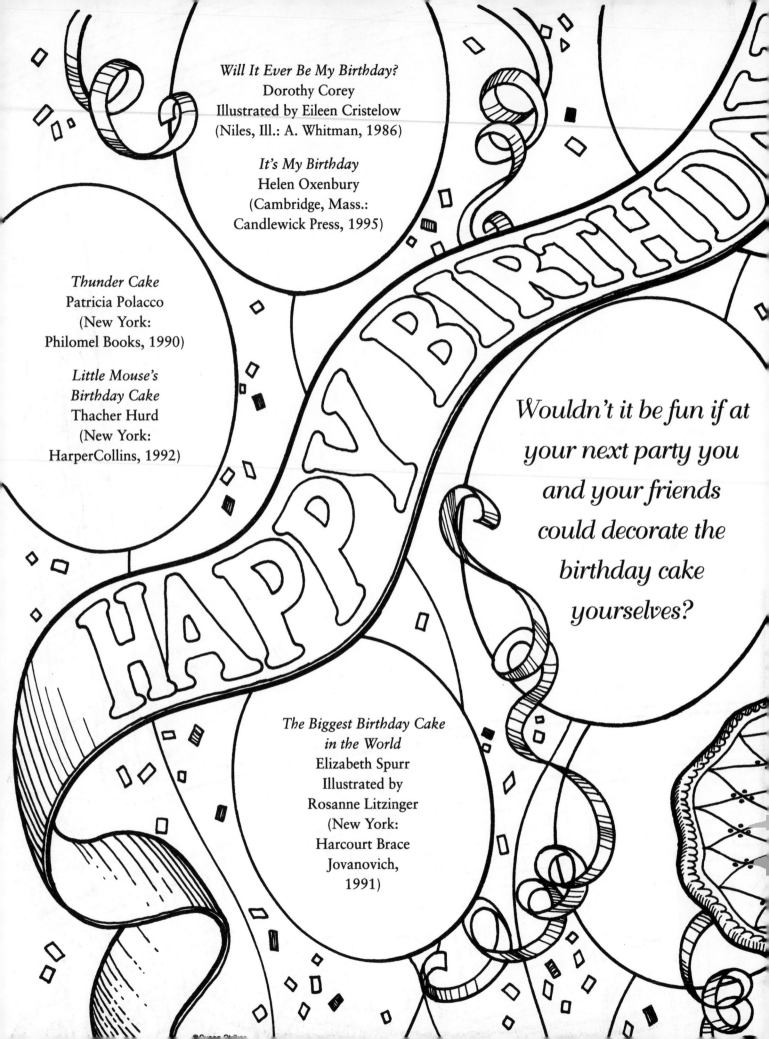

Will It Ever Be My Birthday?
Dorothy Corey
Illustrated by Eileen Cristelow
(Niles, Ill.: A. Whitman, 1986)

It's My Birthday
Helen Oxenbury
(Cambridge, Mass.:
Candlewick Press, 1995)

Thunder Cake
Patricia Polacco
(New York:
Philomel Books, 1990)

*Little Mouse's
Birthday Cake*
Thacher Hurd
(New York:
HarperCollins, 1992)

*The Biggest Birthday Cake
in the World*
Elizabeth Spurr
Illustrated by
Rosanne Litzinger
(New York:
Harcourt Brace
Jovanovich,
1991)

HAPPY BIRTHDAY

*Wouldn't it be fun if at
your next party you
and your friends
could decorate the
birthday cake
yourselves?*

JOB APPLICATION

Name:_____

Job description: _____
_____
_____
_____
_____
_____
_____
_____

Salary required: _____

Benefits requested: _____

Your special qualifications for this job:_____
_____
_____
_____
_____

Experience in this field: _____

Tell us why you think you should be hired: _____
_____
_____
_____

The Lemonade Parade
Ben Brooks
Illustrated by Bill Flavin
(Morton Grove, Ill.: A. Whitman, 1992)

Chicken Man
Michelle Edwards
(New York: William Morrow, 1991)

**On Labor Day we pay our respects to working people.
Picture yourself at the ideal job for you.**

ook of Life

Happy New Year, Beni
Story and pictures by
Jane Breskin Zalben
New York: Henry Holt, 1993)

*The World's Birthday: A Rosh
Hashanah Story*
Barbara Diamond Goldin
Illustrated by
Jeanette Winter
(New York:
Harcourt Brace
Jovanovich, 1990)

On Rosh Hashanah, a person's future is inscribed in the Book of Life.
What do you hope the coming year holds for you?

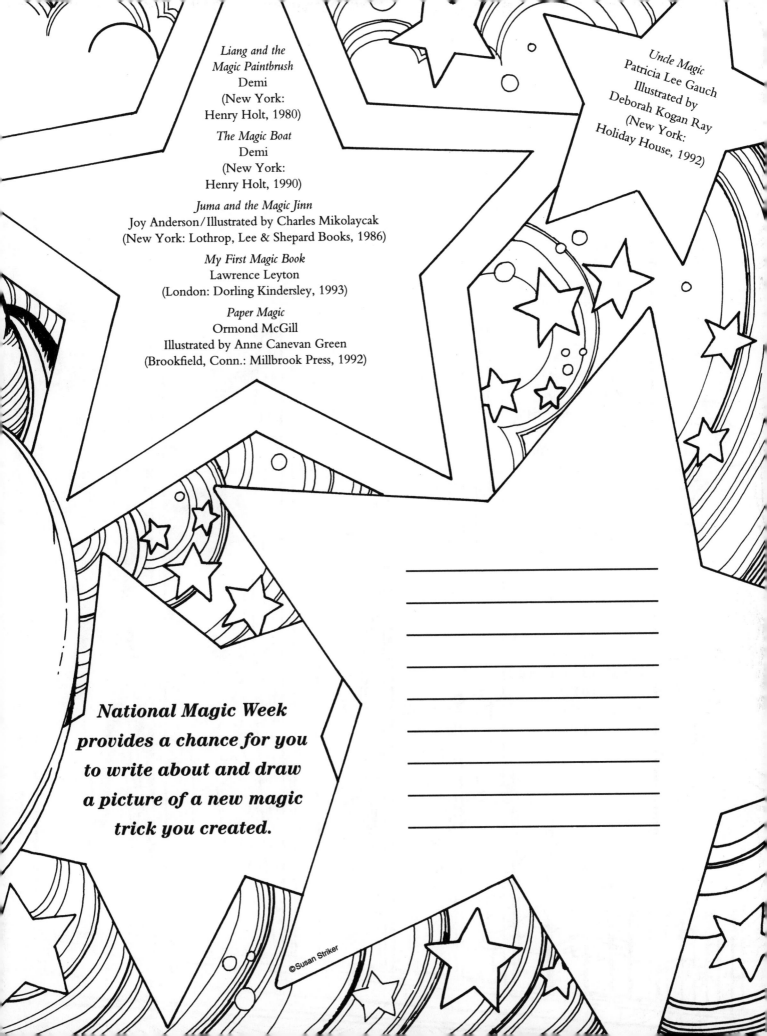

*Liang and the
Magic Paintbrush*
Demi
(New York:
Henry Holt, 1980)

The Magic Boat
Demi
(New York:
Henry Holt, 1990)

Juma and the Magic Jinn
Joy Anderson/Illustrated by Charles Mikolaycak
(New York: Lothrop, Lee & Shepard Books, 1986)

My First Magic Book
Lawrence Leyton
(London: Dorling Kindersley, 1993)

Paper Magic
Ormond McGill
Illustrated by Anne Canevan Green
(Brookfield, Conn.: Millbrook Press, 1992)

Uncle Magic
Patricia Lee Gauch
Illustrated by
Deborah Kogan Ray
(New York:
Holiday House, 1992)

**National Magic Week
provides a chance for you
to write about and draw
a picture of a new magic
trick you created.**

©Susan Striker

United Nations Day
Olive Rabe
Illustrated by Aliki
(New York: Thomas Y.
Crowell, 1965)

*For Every Child a
Better World*
Kermit the Frog
In cooperation with the
United Nations
as told to Louise Gikow
and Ellen Weiss
Illustrated by Bruce
McNally
(Racine, Wis.: Western
Pub., 1993)

*Dear World:
"How I'd put the world
right" by the children of
over 50 nations*
Edited by Richard and
Helen Exley
(New York: Methuen,
1979)

United Nations Day is October 18. The UN is admitting a new member country to celebrate, and you have been asked to design the emerging country's new flag.

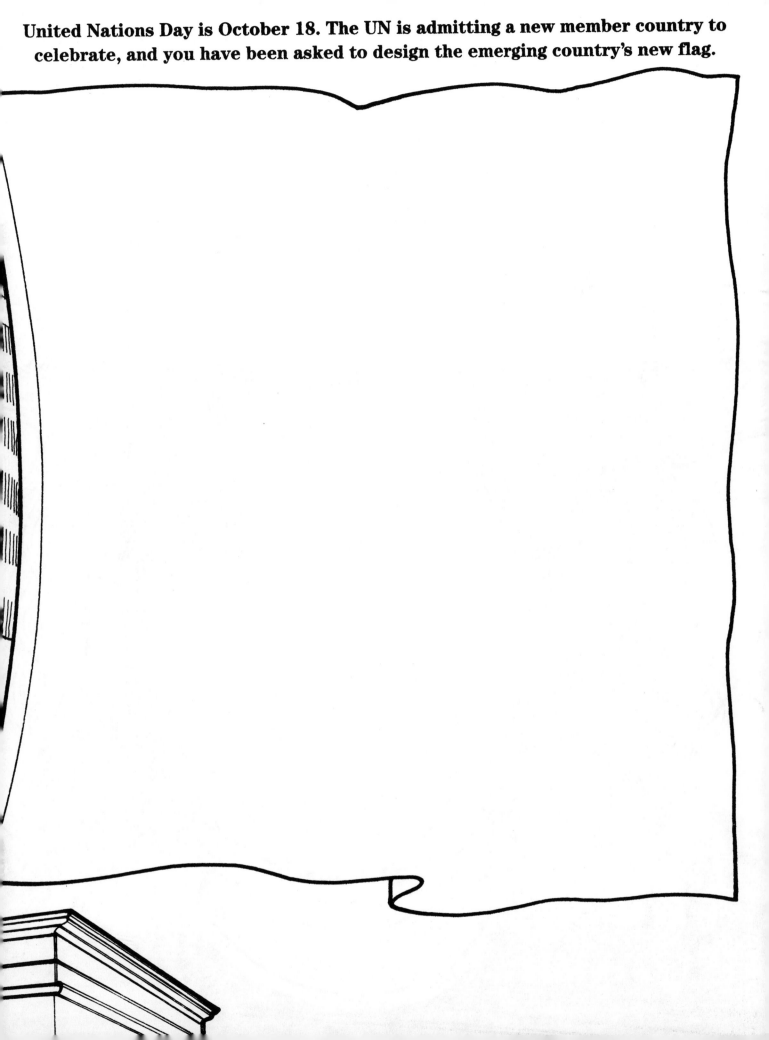

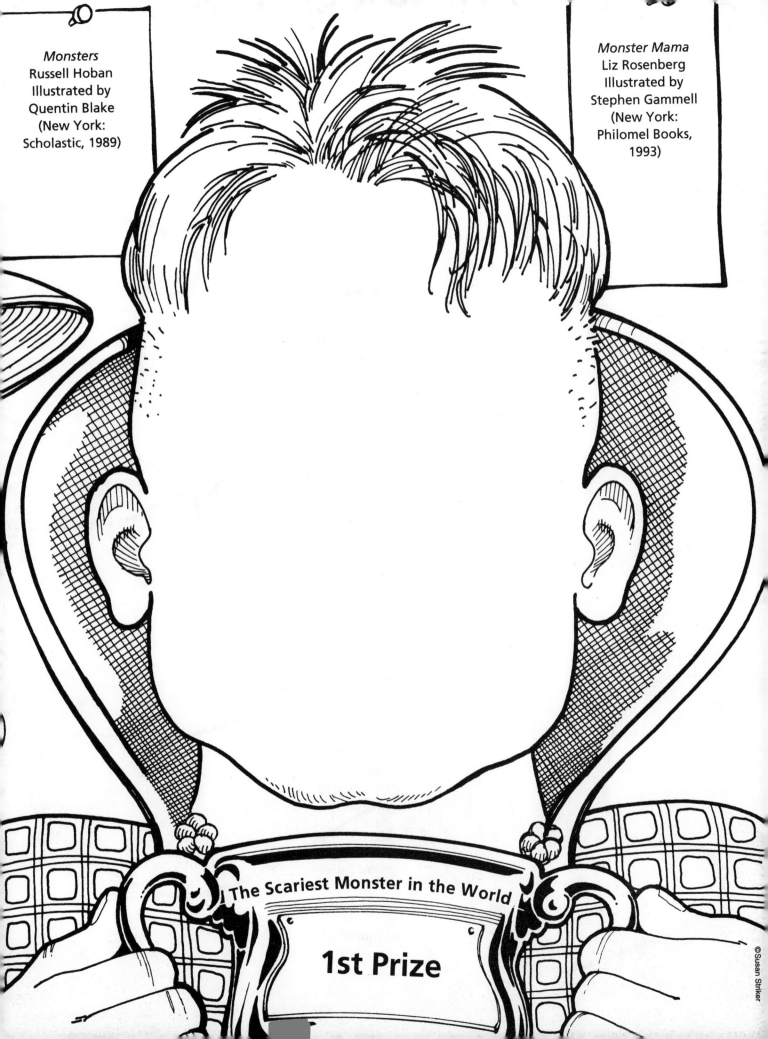

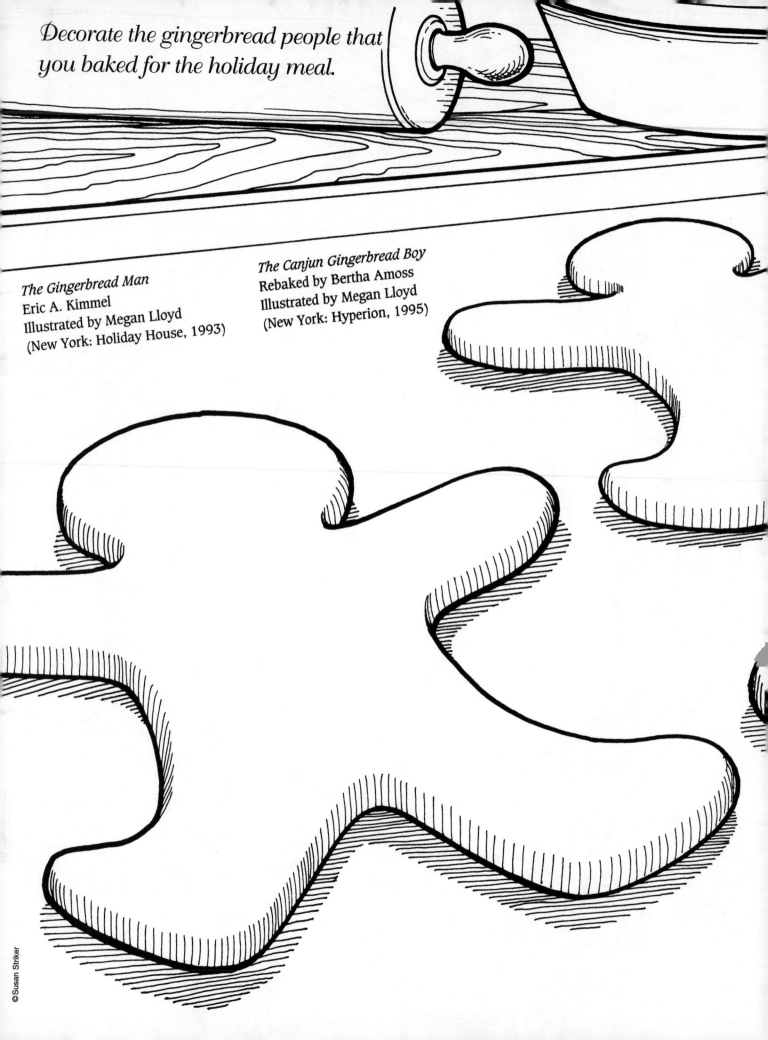

Decorate the gingerbread people that you baked for the holiday meal.

The Gingerbread Man
Eric A. Kimmel
Illustrated by Megan Lloyd
(New York: Holiday House, 1993)

The Canjun Gingerbread Boy
Rebaked by Bertha Amoss
Illustrated by Megan Lloyd
(New York: Hyperion, 1995)

©Susan Striker

Daisy's
Crazy Thanksgiving
Margery Cuyler
Illustrated by Robin Kramer
(New York: Henry Holt, 1992)

©Susan Striker

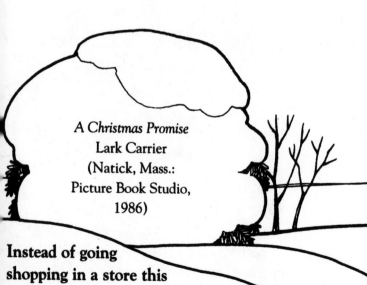

A Christmas Promise
Lark Carrier
(Natick, Mass.:
Picture Book Studio,
1986)

**Instead of going
shopping in a store this
year, use only things Mother Nature
has created as Christmas tree decorations.
While you are at it, see if you can think of gifts
Mother Nature can provide to put under the tree.**

Day one celebrates united families and communities. Draw your family doing a joint activity.

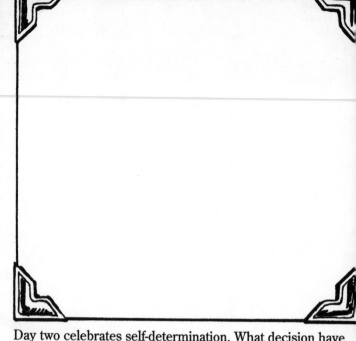

Day two celebrates self-determination. What decision have you made all by yourself?

Kwanzaa is a seven-day nonreligious celebration of black life and black history.

On day five we think about spiritually improving our community. Think of a way to make your community richer.

Day six is dedicated to letting out the artist in all of us. What can you do to celebrate beauty?

Day three celebrates work we do together as a community. Picture a group you belong to engaging in a community activity.

On day four we think about our economic goals. What are you saving money for?

Celebrating Kwanzaa
Diane Hoyt-Goldsmith
Photographs by Lawrence Migdale
(New York: Holiday House, 1993)

Seven Candles for Kwanzaa
Andrea Davis Pinckney
Pictures by Brian Pinckney
(New York: Dial Books for Young
Readers, 1993)

Kwanzaa
A. P. Porter
Illustrated by Janice Lee Porter
(Minneapolis:
Carolrhoda Books, 1991)

Day seven celebrates pride in oneself. What have you done to make you proud of yourself?

Thank You, Santa
Margaret Wild
Illustrated by Kerry Argent
(New York: Scholastic, 1991)

What do you think Santa would like you to give him?

Santa's Wish List

Santa needs new transportation because his sled is so old-fashioned.
Design the newest way to deliver gifts this Christmas Eve.

*Harvey Slumfenburger's
Christmas Present*
John Burningham
(Cambridge, Mass.:
Candlewick Press, 1993)

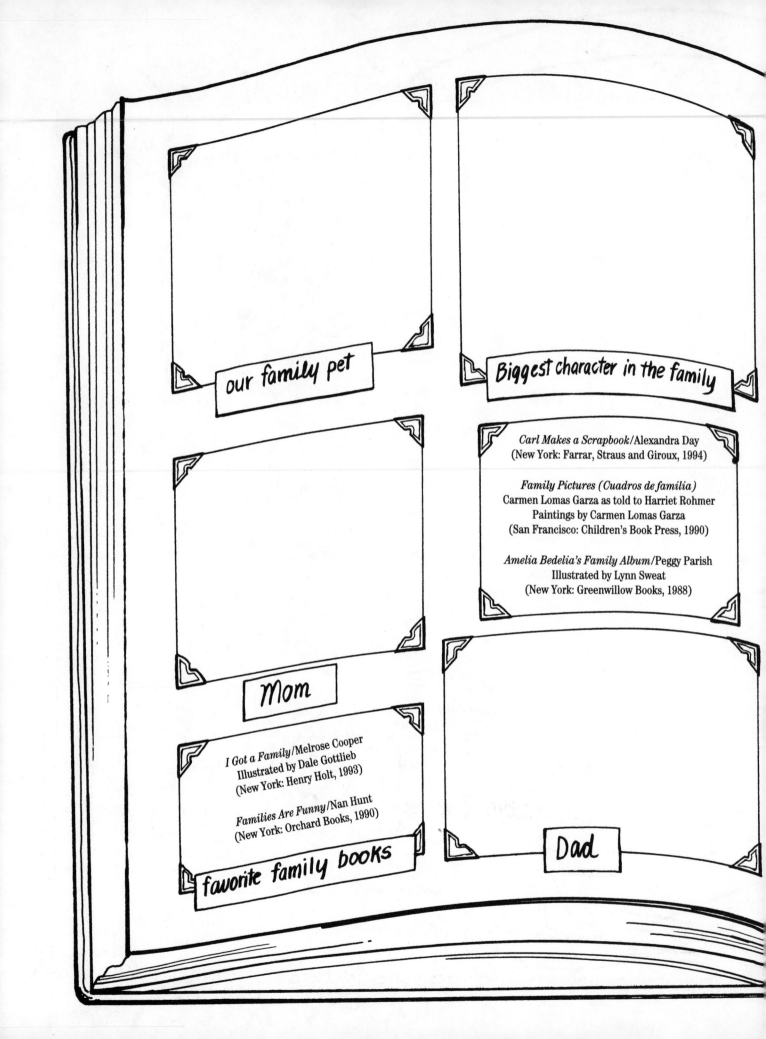

our family pet

Biggest character in the family

Carl Makes a Scrapbook/Alexandra Day
(New York: Farrar, Straus and Giroux, 1994)

Family Pictures (Cuadros de familia)
Carmen Lomas Garza as told to Harriet Rohmer
Paintings by Carmen Lomas Garza
(San Francisco: Children's Book Press, 1990)

Amelia Bedelia's Family Album/Peggy Parish
Illustrated by Lynn Sweat
(New York: Greenwillow Books, 1988)

Mom

I Got a Family/Melrose Cooper
Illustrated by Dale Gottlieb
(New York: Henry Holt, 1993)

Families Are Funny/Nan Hunt
(New York: Orchard Books, 1990)

favorite family books

Dad

For National Family Week let's make a family album.

all of us together

newest addition to our family